Gallery Books
Editor: Peter Fallon

LOVERS

Brian Friel

LOVERS
WINNERS · LOSERS

Gallery Books

This edition of
Lovers
was first published by
The Gallery Press in 1984.
Reprinted in 1987, 1990, and 1993

The Gallery Press
Loughcrew
Oldcastle
County Meath
Ireland

ISBN 0 904011 64 X (*paperback*)
     0 904011 65 8 (*clothbound*)

    The Gallery Press receives financial assistance from An Chomh-
airle Ealaíon / The Arts Council, Ireland.

In memory of
Tyrone Guthrie

Lovers was first performed at the Gate Theatre, Dublin, on Tuesday 18 July, 1967. Direction and lighting were by Hilton Edwards, the décor by Robert Heade, and the cast was as follows:

Winners

MAN	Niall Toibin
WOMAN	Anna Manahan
MAG	Fionnuala Flanagan
JOE	Eamonn Morrissey

Losers

ANDY	Niall Toibin
HANNA	Anna Manahan
CISSIE CASSIDY	Ruth Durley
MRS WILSON	Cathleen Delany

Characters

Winners	*Losers*
MAN	ANDY TRACEY
WOMAN	HANNA WILSON / TRACEY
MAG	MRS WILSON
JOE	CISSY CASSIDY

Winners

EPISODE ONE

When the curtain rises, a MAN *and a* WOMAN *are seated on two high-backed chairs, one down left and one down right, at the edge of the stage. They are the Commentators. They are in their late fifties and carefully dressed in good dark clothes. Each has a book on his knee — not a volume, preferably a bound manuscript — and they read from this every so often. Their reading is impersonal, completely without emotion: their function is to give information. At no time must they reveal an attitude to their material.*

Between them and slightly upstage is Ardnageeha, the hill that overlooks the town of Ballymore. For this I would suggest a large pentagonal platform, approached by four or five shallow steps all round. This is the only stage furniture.

MAG *is seventeen, bubbling with life, inclined to be extreme in her enthusiasms. Although she is not really very beautiful, her vivacity gives her a distinct attraction. Whatever she likes, she loves; whatever she dislikes, she hates — momentarily. She is either very elated or very depressed, but no emotion is ever permanent. She wears a blue school blazer, white blouse, grey skirt.*

JOE *is seventeen and a half. He is a serious boy, a good student, interested in his books. He is at the age when he is earnest about life; and he has a total and touching belief in the value and importance of education.*

TIME: *The present in Ireland.*

MAN   At approximately 9:45 on the morning of Saturday, June 4, 1966, Margaret Mary Enright set out from her home, a detached red-brick house on the outskirts of the town of Ballymore, County Tyrone, Northern Ireland. Before she left, she brought breakfast to her mother, who was still in bed; and as she passed her father's surgery, which is built as an annex to the house, she tapped with the back of her fingers on the frosted glass panel of the door. In a small attaché case she had her schoolbooks and sandwiches for lunch. She cycled through the town and at High Street she met two friends and stopped to talk to them: Joan O'Hara, a classmate, and Philip Moran. They told her they planned to go boating on Lough Gorm that afternoon and asked her to join them. She said that perhaps she would. Then she cycled out the Mill Road until she came to Whelan's Brae. There she left the road and pushed her bicycle —

MAG *enters at this point.*

— across the fields until she came to the foot of Ardnageeha, the hill that overlooks the town of Bally-more. She left her bicycle at the bottom of Ardnageeha, and climbed to the top. It was a glorious summer's morning. Temperatures were in the lower seventies. And there was no wind.

When MAG gets to the top of the hill, she looks around for JOE. He has not arrived yet. She lights a cigarette, squats on the ground, and waits for him.

WOMAN At roughly the same time as Margaret Enright set out, Joseph Michael Brennan left his home at 37 Railway Terrace. His mother had gone to work two hours previously and had left his breakfast ready for him. His father was still in bed and asleep.

He went out through the back yard, down the mews lane, and across the waste ground between the rear of Railway Terrace and the railway line. On his way across the waste ground he met some children who were throwing stones at rats. He followed the line out past the marshalling yard, under the iron bridge, and for a mile out into the country. He carried his schoolbooks in a leather satchel. When he got to the level crossing he cut across the fields until he came to the foot of Ardnageeha, the hill that overlooks the town of Ballymore.

JOE *enters here.*

Then he climbed to the top.

MAG *sees him coming up the hill. She goes down the far side, i.e., upstage, until she is out of sight. There she hides.*

MAN Margaret Enright was a pupil of Saint Mary's Grammar School, run by the Sisters of Mercy. And Joseph Brennan was a pupil of Saint Kevin's College, a grammar school for boys run by the clergy of the diocese. She was seventeen; he seventeen and a half. And they had their books with them because school was officially over for the year and they planned to spend the day studying for their final examinations at the end of their grammar school course. The examinations began the following Wednesday.

JOE Maggie! Maggie! (*Shouts*) Maaaaaag!

When he gets no response, he squats on the ground, opens his bag, takes out a book, and begins to work.

WOMAN They stayed on top of Ardnageeha, that overlooks the town of Ballymore, from ten until two. They had their lunch up there. We can assume that they did some work because Joseph was an excellent student, not brilliant, but very keen and very industrious. Margaret was no scholar. She was intelligent but scattered. And we can assume that they talked some and perhaps dreamed some, because they were young and the day was beautiful. And even though the examinations were imminent, they cannot have been all that important to the young pair, who were to be married in exactly three weeks' time, on Saturday, June 25, because Margaret was pregnant.

13

JOE *glances up from his work and scans the land below him. No sign of* MAGGIE. *He returns to his book. Now* MAGGIE *creeps up behind him and pounces on his back, trying to push him to the edge of the hill so that he will roll down. They wrestle for a few seconds.*

JOE Come on! Cut it out, will you! That'll do!

MAG Ha! You leaped like a rabbit!

JOE I was looking for you. Where were you?

MAG Waiting for you. You're late.

JOE I was here at ten exactly.

MAG I've been here for at least half an hour.

She throws herself on the ground in exaggerated exhaustion, produces cigarettes, and begins talking. During most of this episode JOE *is studying, or trying to study. But occasionally he tunes in to her prattle. By throwing in an occasional word he gives her the impression he is conversing with her.*

JOE Did you walk it?

MAG The bike's lying at the foot of the hill.

JOE I didn't see it.

MAG Sure you're half blind! God, my tongue's hanging out for a week after that! (*Inhales and exhales with satisfaction*) Aaah, bliss! Sister Pascal says: You may search the lists of the canonized but you will search in vain for the saint that smoked. Maybe you'll be a saint, Joe.

JOE Let's get started.

MAG I read in a book that there are one million two hundred thousand nuns in the world. Isn't that fierce? Imagine if they were all gathered in one place — on an island, say — and the Chinese navy was let loose at them — cripes, you'd hear the squeals in Tobermore! I have a wicked mind, too. D'you ever think things like that, Joe? I'm sure you don't. I think that women have far more corrupt minds than men, but I think that men are more easily corrupted than women.

JOE We'll get a couple of hours done before we eat.

MAG (*With excessive disgust*) Food! — I don't care if I never see another bite ever again. My God, I thought I was going to vomit my guts out this morning! And this could keep up for the next seven months, according to Doctor Watson. The only consolation is that *you're* all right. It would be wild altogether if you were at it too. Sympathetic sickness, they call it. But it's only husbands get it. Maybe you'll get it this day three weeks — the minute we get married — God, wouldn't that be a scream! D'you know what Joan O'Hara told me? That all the time her mother was expecting Oliver Plunkett, her father never lifted his head out of the kitchen sink. Isn't it crazy! And for the last three days he lay squealing on the floor like a stuck pig and her mother had to get the police for him in the end. I love this view of Ballymore: the town and the fields and the lake; and the people. When I'm up here and look down on them, I want to run down and hug them all and kiss them. But then when I'm down among them I feel like doing that (*she cocks a snook into* JOE's *face*) into their faces. I bet you that's how God feels at times, too. Wouldn't you think so?

JOE I don't know how God feels.

MAG Why not?

JOE Because I'm not God.

MAG Oh, you're so clever! Well, I'll tell you something: there are occasions in my life when *I* know how God feels.

JOE Good for you.

MAG And one of those occasions is now. (*Puffing her cigarette regally*) At this moment God feels . . . expansive . . . and beneficent . . . and philanthropy.

JOE Philanthropic.

MAG (*After momentary setback*) And we will not be put into bad humour by grubby little pedants.

JOE Look, Mag: we came up here to study. What are you going to do first?

MAG French. And then maths. And then Spanish. And then English language and literature. After lunch geography and history of the world. I have planned a programme for myself. The important thing about revising for an examination is to have a method. What are you starting with?

JOE Maths.

MAG Then what?

JOE That's all.

MAG Only maths?

JOE Huh-huh.

> *She considers this absurd idea for a second. Then, because* JOE *is wiser in these things than she, she readily agrees with him.*

MAG Then that's what I'll do too. (*Really worried*) My God, if the volume of a cone doesn't come up, I'm scootrified! Not that I care — I can afford to go down in one subject. (*Pause*) Joe . . .

JOE What?

MAG What's the real difference between language and literature?

JOE You're not serious, Maggie!

MAG Don't — don't — don't tell me . . . I remember now . . . One is talking and the other is . . . books!

JOE Talking . . . ?

MAG That's it.

JOE That's no definition! Language is —

MAG Don't say another word. I have it in my head. But if you start lecturing, I'll lose it again. I have my own way of remembering things. Joe, last night again Papa asked me to let him get the flat painted for us before we move in.

JOE (*Doggedly*) I said I'll paint the flat.

MAG That's what I told him. And I was thinking, Joe . . .

JOE What?

MAG If we put a lace curtain across the kitchen window, we wouldn't actually *see* down into the slaughterhouse yard.

JOE And if we wore earplugs all the time, we wouldn't actually *hear* the mooing and the shooting!

MAG (*Softly to herself*) And even if a curtain did make the room darker, it'd still be lovely.

JOE I signed the lease yesterday evening.

MAG (*Absolutely thrilled*) It's ours now? We own it?

JOE Old Kerrigan was so busy working he wouldn't take time off to go into the office; so we put the document on the back of a cow that was about to be shot and that's where we signed it. Cockeyed old miser!

MAG He's not!

JOE What?

MAG Cockeyed.

JOE I'm telling you. And crazy, too. In a big rubber apron and him dripping with blood. And cows and sheep and bullocks dropping dead all around him.

MAG Oh God, my stomach!

JOE *realizes that his tale is successful. He gets up on his feet to enact the scene.* MAG *listens with delight and soon gets drawn into the pantomime.*

JOE 'Drive them up there! Another beast. Come on! Come on! I haven't all day. And what's bothering you, young Brennan? Steady, there! Steady! Bang! Bang! Drag it away! Slit its throat! Slice it open! Skin it!'

MAG Stop — stop!

JOE 'Another beast! Get a move on! What am I paying you fellas for?' You told me to call about the flat, Mr. Kerrigan. 'Steady — bang! Bang! Damnit, I nearly missed — bang! — that's it. Drag him off. What are you saying, young Brennan? The lease? Oh, the lease! Oh, aye. Here we are.' (JOE *produces an imaginary document from his hip pocket*) 'Best flat in town. Hell, it's all blood now.' (JOE *wipes the imaginary document on his leg*) 'Come on! Another animal! There's a fine beast for you, young Brennan! Look at those shanks! Bang! Bang! Never knew what hit him! I sign here, son, don't I?' (JOE *pretends to write: but the pen does not work and he flings it away*) 'Hell, that doesn't write.'

MAG Bang! Bang!

JOE 'Keep behind me, young Brennan. This is a dangerous job.'

MAG Let's sign it in blood, young Brennan.

JOE 'Finest view in town. And the noise down here's great company. Bang! Bang!'

MAG Like living in Dead Man's Creek.

JOE There's a bullock that looks like the president of Saint

Kevin's. Bang! Bang!

MAG A sheep the image of Sister Paul. Bang! Bang!

JOE Drag 'em away!

MAG Slice 'em open!

JOE Joan O'Hara's white poodle, Tweeny.

MAG Bang! And Philip Moran's mother.

JOE Bang! Bang! Doctor Watson.

MAG A friend. Pass, friend, pass.

JOE Skinny Skeehan, the solicitor.

MAG Bang-bang-bang-bang! Look — Reverend Mother!

JOE Where?

MAG To the right — behind the rocks!

JOE (*Calling sweetly*) Mother Dolores.

MAG (*Answering sweetly*) Yes, Joseph?

JOE (*Viciously*) Bang-bang-bang!

MAG *grabs her stomach and falls slowly.*

MAG Into thy hands, O Lord —

JOE Bang!

The final bullet enters her shoulder.

MAG O shite —!

MAG *rolls on the ground, helpless with laughter.*

JOE The town clerk — bang! All the teachers — bang!

MAG The church choir —

JOE Bang! Everyone that lives along snobby, snotty Melville Road — bang-bang-bang-bang-bang!

MAG A holy-cost, by God.

JOE *listens attentively. Silence.*

JOE Everything's quiet. Now we'll have peace to study. Back to the books.

MAG I'm sore all over. (*Searching*) Give us a fag quick.

JOE (*Bashfully*) I'm afraid — I — sort of — sort of lost my head there, ma'am.

MAG Does your mother know you act the clown like that?

JOE Does your father know you smoke? Look at the time it is! I came here to work.

> *He goes back to his books. He is immediately immersed.*

MAG Joe . . .

JOE What?

MAG The flat's ours now?

JOE Isn't that what I'm telling you.

MAG You're sure you wouldn't like the top floor in our house?

JOE Positive.

MAG (*After a moment's hesitation*) So am I. I just wanted to know if you were, too.

JOE Goodbye.

MAG It's only that Papa'll be lonely without me. For his sake, really. But he'll get over that. And it's just that this is the first time he'll ever have been separated from me, even for a night. But he'll get over it. All parents have to face it sooner or later. (*Happily*) Besides, I can wheel the pram over every afternoon. (*She looks at* JOE, *lost in his books: and again she has the momentary dread of the exam*) I'm like you, Joe. When I concentrate, you could yell at me and I wouldn't hear you. (*She opens a book — almost at random. Looks at the sky*) It's going to be very warm . . . (*She takes off her school blazer, rolls up the sleeves of her blouse, and stretches out under the sun*) If we didn't have to work, we could sun-bathe. (*Pause*) That Easter we were in Florence, I kept thinking about your father and how good the sun there would have been for his asthma. I read in a book that asthma is purely psychosomatic and that a man with asthma has a mother-fixation. Crazy the things they dig up too. I'm glad Papa's not a doctor or he'd be watching me for symptoms all the time. Your parents are such wonderful people, Joe. I'm crazy about them. And I'm going to model myself on your mother. And from now on I'm going to treat my own parents with . . . with a certain dignity. My God, the things they said to me — they seared my soul forever —

And without drawing a breath she hums a few bars of a popular song. She has a book before her eyes — but her eyes are closed.

MAN   Joseph Brennan was the only child of Mick and Nora Brennan. Because of his asthma, Mick Brennan has not had a job for over twenty years. He receives unemployment benefit and this is supplemented by the earnings of his wife, who works as a charwoman from 8.00 a.m. until 8.00 p.m., six days a week, for two and six an hour. In a good week her wages come to around nine pounds. She has one hundred and thirteen pounds ten shillings and sixpence in post-office savings and three pounds five shillings and sevenpence in an ornate tea caddy in the kitchen. She is a quiet woman, and all her dreams and love and hope and delight were centred unashamedly in Joe.

  Mick Brennan — or Mick the Moocher, as he is known in Ballymore — is keenly interested in horses, greyhounds, ferrets, and pigeons. He spends most of his day at the greyhound track. To his friends he talked a lot about Joe, always referring to him in a casual, disparaging way as The Lad.

  Nora Brennan has no hobbies.

WOMAN   Margaret Enright was the daughter of Walter and Beth Enright. Walter is a dentist. When he married, he was the only dentist in Ballymore. Now there are three; and his practice is the smallest. As a young man he was interested in books and travel and music. Now, after his work, he sits at home, and drinks, and reads thrillers. Beth, his wife, has been under Doctor Watson's care for seventeen years, ever since the death of her infant son. She gave birth to twins — Margaret and Peter — and five days after the birth Peter was discovered in his cot, smothered by a pillow. She never fully recovered from this. In her good days she is carefree — almost reckless. In her bad days she wears dark glasses and lies in bed. Walter looks after her constantly.

MAG *is drowsy with the heat. Her head is propped against her case. Through slitted eyes she surveys the scene below in Ballymore. She is addressing* JOE *but knows that he is not listening to her.*

MAG I can see the boarders out on the tennis courts. They should be studying. And there's a funeral going up High Street; nine cars, and a petrol lorry, and an ambulance. Maybe the deceased was run over by the petrol lorry — the father of a large family — and the driver is paying his respects and crying his eyes out. If he doesn't stop blubbering, he'll run over someone else. And the widow is in the ambulance, all in plaster, crippled for life. (*She tries out a mime of this — both arms and legs cast in awkward shapes*) And the children are going to be farmed out to cruel aunts with squints and moustaches. Sister Michael has a beard. Joan O'Hara says she shaves with a cut-throat every first Friday and uses an after-shave lotion called Virility. God, nuns are screams if you don't take them seriously. I think I'd rather be a widow than a widower; but I'd rather be a bachelor than a spinster. And I'd rather be deaf than dumb; but I'd rather be dumb than blind. And if I had to choose between lung cancer, a coronary, and multiple sclerosis, I'd take the coronary. Papa's family all died of coronaries, long before they were commonplace. (*She sits up to tell the following piece of family history*) He had a sister, Nan, who used to sing at the parochial concert every Christmas; and one year, when she was singing *Jerusalem* — you know, just before the chorus, when the piano is panting Huh-huh-huh-huh-huh-huh, she opened her mouth and dropped like a log . . .

Joe, d'you think (*quoting something she has read*) my legs have got thick, my body gross, my facial expression passive to dull, and my eyes lack-lustre? I hope it's a boy, and that it'll be like you — with a great big bursting brain. Or maybe it'll be twins — like me. I wonder what Peter would have been like? Sometimes when she's very ill Mother calls me Peter. If it were going to be twins I'd rather have a boy and a girl than two boys or two girls;

but if it were going to be triplets I'd rather have two boys and a girl or two girls and a boy than three boys or three girls. (*Very wisely and directed to* JOE) And I have a feeling it's going to be premature.

> JOE *is alerted. His eyes move away from his book, but his head does not move.*

Mothers have intuitions about these things. We were premature. Five weeks. Very tricky.

JOE Tricky?

MAG Caesarean, as a matter of fact.

> JOE *has never heard the term.*

JOE (*Too casually*) That — sure — sure that's — so was I too.

MAG (*Delighted*) Were you? Isn't that marvellous! We really have everything in common! Oh, Joe, wait till you hear: I was doing my hair this morning, and d'you know what I found in the comb? A grey hair! I'm old! Two months pregnant and I'm as grey as a badger! Isn't it a scream! I think a young face and silver hair is more attractive than an old face and black hair. But if I had to choose between a young face and black hair and an old face and silver hair I think I'd prefer the young face. (*Gently*) You have a young face. You're only a boy. You're only a baby really. I'll have two babies to take care of. (*She touches his shoe*) Joe, we'll be happy, Joe, won't we? It's such a beautiful morning. So still. I think this is the most important moment in my life. And I think (*she laughs with embarrassment*), I think sometimes that happiness, real happiness, was never discovered until we discovered it. Isn't that silly? And I want to share it with everyone — everywhere.

JOE Stupid.

MAG What?

JOE A fat lot you have to give.

MAG I didn't say give!

JOE You did!

MAG I did not!

JOE I heard you!

MAG Liar! I said 'share'!

JOE Share what?

MAG You wouldn't understand!

JOE Understand what?

MAG has lost the thread of the argument.

MAG Anything! 'Cos you're just a selfish, cold, horrible, priggish, conceited donkey! Stuck in your old books as if they were the most important thing in the world; and your — your — your intended waiting like a dog for you to toss her a kind word!

JOE I only asked.

MAG You hate me — that's it — you're going to marry me just to crush me! I've heard of men like you — sadicists! I've read about them in books! But I never thought for a second —

She breaks off suddenly and clasps her stomach in terrified agony. At the same time she is pleasantly aware of JOE'S mounting panic.

MAG Oh, my God — !

JOE What?

MAG Oooooooooh —!

JOE What — what — what is it, Maggie?

MAG Joe —!

JOE Mag, are you sick? Are you sick, Mag?

MAG (*Formally*) Labour has commenced.

JOE (*In panic*) Sweet God! How d'you know? What's happening? I'll get help! Don't move! Doctor Watson warned you to stop cycling! How d'you feel? I'll carry you. Don't move — don't move!

In total consternation he searches her face, noting every flicker of every feature. She is gratified at his anxiety. She acts the brave sufferer.

MAG I . . . think —

JOE Don't talk! Don't move! Where did you leave your bike?

MAG Stay with me, Joe, please. Hold my hand.

JOE God, this is fierce! On top of a bloody hill! You're all right, Mag, aren't you? Aren't you all right?

MAG (*She gives him a brave smile*) Dear Joe. I'm fine, thank you, Joe.

JOE What's happening? Tell me.

MAG Nothing to be alarmed about. False pains.

JOE False . . .?

MAG (*Cheerily*) Gone again. For the time being.

JOE They'll be back?

MAG Oh, yes. But maybe not for a month.

JOE God, I'm not worth tuppence.

MAG I'm sorry for calling you names.

JOE Maybe you should go home, Mag, eh?

MAG I'm fine. Really. Go on with your work.

JOE God, I don't know.

MAG (*Smiling reassuringly*) Please. I'll just rest.

> JOE *gropes for something tender to say. But he is too embarrassed.*

JOE Maggie, I'll . . . I'll try . . . I'll try to be —

MAG (*A revelation*) I know now!

JOE Huh?

MAG No breakfast!

JOE What are you —?

MAG Hunger pangs! That's what it was! I'm ravenous!

JOE Hunger —?

MAG I could eat the side of a horse!

JOE But you said you didn't care —?

MAG Don't be always quoting what I said. There's nothing as detestable as being quoted. I change my mind every two minutes. Or would you rather it was labour?

JOE (*Totally baffled*) I . . . I . . . (*Resolutely*) I'm going to work.

> *He begins to study again.* MAG *opens her case and takes out a packet of sandwiches.*

MAG All the same, if I eat now, I'll have nothing left for later.
I'll do with two small sandwiches. Three. (*Eats vigor-
ously*) My big regret now is that I dropped domestic
science in junior. Can't even remember how to make
rock buns. And poor old Dorothy Quilty was so sweet to
us all. Did I ever tell you what happened to her, Joe?
(*She waits for a reply, gets none, and goes on anyhow*)
She was from Dublin. And one afternoon, during the
Christmas holidays, she went to the pictures. And this
man sat in the seat beside her — gospel truth — Joan
O'Hara heard it from a cousin of hers who's a guard in
Dundalk. And anyhow during the film this fellow gave
her an injection in the arm. Of course no one saw him.
And when she passed out he carried her out to the street,
and his accomplice was waiting there in a car, and they
drove off with her. (*Waits again for* JOE's *reaction. Then
goes on*) And four days later she was found in the
Wicklow mountains — up a sycamore tree.

        JOE *turns round slowly to face her.*

JOE What d'you mean — up a sycamore tree?
MAG Hiding.
JOE Hiding what?
MAG Herself. In the leaves.
JOE (*Deliberately*) You really are crazy.
MAG She was hiding in the leaves, stupid, because they had
taken her clothes away — that's the way. And for your
knowledge and information, she had to give up teaching
after that experience. Nervous . . . Nervosity; that's what
the doctor said she had. And she's now a stitcher in a
Belfast shirt factory — of all girls.
JOE For a woman that's going to be married in four weeks'
time —
MAG Three.
JOE Honest to God, the stories that you come out with —
juvenile, that's the only word for them. And I'm trying to
work at integration. So will you shut up?
MAG (*With dignity*) I will. I certainly will. And the next time I
break breath with you, you'll be a chastened man. (*Brief*

pause) But before I go silent for the rest of the day, there's something I want to get clear between us, Joseph Brennan. (*Pause*) Joe.

JOE   What?

MAG   You never proposed to me.

JOE   Huh?

MAG   You haven't *asked* me to marry you.

JOE   What are you raving about?

MAG   Propose to me.

JOE   God!

MAG   Now.

JOE   You really are —!

MAG   Ask me.

JOE   Will-you-marry-me. Now!

MAG   Thank you, Joseph. I will.

He goes back to his books.

JOE   Bats! Raving bloody bats!

MAG   The children will want to know. Especially the girls. And I'll tell them it was a beautiful morning in June, a Saturday, four days before the exams began, on top of Ardnageeha, the Hill of the Wind. And everything was still. And their father said, 'Maggie,' very shyly, 'Maggie Enright, will you make me the proudest and happiest man in the whole world? Will you be my spouse?' And I said, 'Joe' — nothing more. And I think that was the most important moment in my life. (*She looks at* JOE, *sees him engrossed in his work, has a sudden stab of anxiety and grabs a book*) I really am scootrified this time! Integration — that's on my course, too — I think. What in the name of God does it mean?

She buries her head in her hands and studies furiously.

MAN   It is estimated that Joe Brennan and Maggie Enright came down from the top of Ardnageeha around two o'clock that afternoon. They were seen walking hand-in-hand along the Mill Road at about ten past two; and ten minutes later they were seen going in the direction of

26

Lough Gòrm, which lies to the east of Ballymore. Both were on foot. Joe was wheeling Maggie's bicycle. The recorded temperature at 3.00 p.m. on that Saturday afternoon, June 4, 1966, was 77 degrees. And there was no wind.

WOMAN Lough Gorm is three miles long and half a mile broad, and there are forty-nine islands of various sizes scattered over it. There are seven boats on the lake. And on that afternoon two of them were out. Philip Moran and Joan O'Hara were out in Mr. O'Hara's boat. They went out at noon and returned at 1.30. The other boat was William Anthony Clerkin's, an accountant in the local bank. He fished from eleven that morning until two that afternoon. Then he pulled in on the south shore, beside the old lime kiln, and went home for his lunch. He left the oars and rowlocks lying in the boat. When he returned an hour and twenty minutes later, the boat was gone; and a girl's bicycle was lying at the edge of the water.

MAG I'll tell you a tip. (*Pause*) Joe. (*Pause*) D'you want to know a clever trick I have, Joe? In all exams the smart thing to do is to write down everything you know — no matter what the question is. Les oiseaux qui en sont dehors désespèrent d'y entrer; et d'un pareil soin en sortir, ceux qui sont au-dedans; if the moving line is at right angles to the plane figure, the prism is a right prism; in 1586 Sir Philip Sidney met his death at Zutphen from a wound in the nether regions of the body; the volume of a cone is $\frac{1}{3}\pi$ dh multiplied by — my God, and that's the one thing I know! Shakespeare, the Bard of Avon, besides writing thirty-four extant plays, was married to a woman eight years his senior, and was the father of twins. Like Papa. As flies to wanton boys are we to the gods; they kill us for their sport. Sister Pascal says that you always know Protestants by their yellow faces and Catholics by their dirty fingernails. (*She rises, moves away from* JOE, *who is lost in his books, and stands at the edge of the hilltop. She looks down over the town*) Nuns are screams — if you don't take them seriously . . . I don't know what things I take seriously . . . Never books or school or things like that . . . Maybe God sometimes, when I'm in trouble . . . and Papa . . . and being a good wife to you . . . It's so quiet, with the whole world before me . . . Joe (*she turns to face him*), Joe, you'll have to talk a lot more to me, Joe. I don't care if it's not sensible talk; it's just that — you know — I feel lonely at times . . . Of course I'll have Joan; she'll visit us; Phil and herself. And you'll like her better when you get to know her. All that's wrong with her is that she's not mature yet; and she can be cruel at times . . .

After we're married we'll have lots of laughs together, Joe, won't we? We'll laugh a lot, won't we? (*She begins to cry inaudibly*) Joe, I'm nervous; I'm frightened, Joe; I'm terrified . . .

MAN At 6.20 William Anthony Clerkin reported to Sergeant Finlay that his boat had been stolen. The Sergeant and Mr. Finlay returned to Lough Gorm and walked around a portion of the south shore. They sighted the upturned boat floating about fifty yards west of the biggest island, Oileán na gCrann.

WOMAN As a result of inquiries, the Sergeant learned that the bicycle belonged to Margaret Mary Enright. He phoned the Enright home and discovered that the girl had left there early in the morning. He then called at the Brennan home and Mr. Brennan informed him that he had not seen his son all day.

MAG I will tell my secrets to my baby.

MAN It was then 7.45 p.m.

WOMAN At 8.10 a search party of twenty-three local men set out to search the forty-nine islands.

MAG *has another twinge of conscience; she plunges into her book again.*

MAG (*Reads*) LP, MQ, and NR are ordinates perpendicular to the axis OX such that LP $=8$", MQ $= 7$", and NR $= 4$". Find the lengths of the ordinates at the midpoints of LM and MN of the circular arc through P, Q, and R, and by means of Simpson's rule and the five ordinates estimate . . . (*Her concentration fails*) Everything's so still. That's what I love. At a time like this, if I close my eyes and scarcely breathe, I sometimes have very important philosophic thoughts — about existence and life and et cetera. That's what people mean when they talk of a woman's intuitions. Every woman has intuitions but I think that pregnant women have more important intuitions than non-pregnant women. And another thing too: a woman's intuitions are more important while she's pregnant than after she's had her baby. So when you see a pregnant woman sitting at the fire, knitting, not talking, you can be sure she's having very important philosophic thoughts about things. I wish to God I could knit. Years and years ago in primary school I began a pair of gloves; but the fingers scootrified me and I turned them into ankle socks . . .

I think your father's a highly intellectual man, really; a born naturalist. And your mother — she's so practical and so unassuming. That's what I want to be. One of these days I'm going to stop talking altogether — for good — and people will say: Didn't Mrs. Joseph Brennan become dignified all of a sudden? Since the baby arrived, I suppose. I think now, Joe, it's going to be nineteen days overdue. And in desperation they'll bring me into the hospital and put me on the treadmill — that's a new yoke they have to bring on labour; Joan told me about it. An aunt of a second cousin of hers was on it non-stop for thirteen hours. They keep you climbing up this big wheel that keeps giving way under you. Just like the slaves in olden times. And after the baby's born they'll keep it in an oxygen tent for a fortnight. And when we get it home it'll have to be fed with an eye dropper every forty-nine minutes and we'll get no sleep at all and — (*Sudden alarming thought*) My God, you won't get asthma like your father when you get old, will you?

JOE . . . equals $2.8 \times t \times p$ all over pv to the power of $1.4 \times v$ . . .

MAG Even if you do, I'll rub your chest with menthol and give you the kiss of life.

JOE Shhhhhh.

She watches him for a moment in silence. He is unaware of her existence.

MAG There's something I want to tell you, Joe, and there's something I want to ask you as well. And I think I'll ask you the thing I want to ask you before I tell you the thing I want to tell you. (*Pause*) Joe.

JOE (*Very irritable*) What-what-what?

MAG My parents sleep in separate rooms. Do yours?

JOE In our house there are two bedrooms. I'm in one of them.

MAG And do they — have a single bed or a double bed?

JOE Double. Satisfied, Nosy?

MAG (*Fully gratified*) I knew that was a real marriage. That's what I want. Like your parents. Joe, there's something I want to try to explain to you, too.

JOE Look — five minutes more — that's all I ask. (*He does not listen to her*)

MAG I look at Papa and Mother, and Mr. and Mrs. O'Hara, and all the other parents and I think — I think — none of them knows what being in love really is. And that's why I think we're different. God, doesn't that sound stupid when you say it! But that's the way I feel, Joe. At this moment — here — now — I'm crazy about you — and mad and reckless, so that I want to shout to the whole town: I love Joe Brennan! I'm mad about him! I'd do anything for him! D'you hear me, Mother Dolores? I love him so much — so much — that I want to — to become him! Isn't that stupid? And when I look around me — at Papa and Mother and the O'Haras — I think: by God we'll never become like that, because — don't laugh at me, Joe — because I think we're unique! Is that how you feel, too?

JOE flings his book from him in exasperation. Speaks very articulately.

JOE You - are - a - bloody - pain - in - the - neck! (*Quickly*) You haven't shut up for five consecutive minutes since we got here! You have done no work yourself and you have wasted my morning, too! And if anyone should be working, it's you, because you haven't a clue about anything! In fact, you're the stupidest person I ever met!

MAG Stewbag!

JOE Sticks and stones — go ahead!

MAG And you can't kick a football the length of yourself!

JOE What has that got to do with it?

MAG That's what everybody calls you 'cos that's all you can do is stew — stew — stew!

JOE Born stupid.

MAG (*Crying*) Stewbag! Stewbag!

JOE Bawl away. Bawl your head off. But if you think I'm going to waste my life in Skinny Skeehan's smelly office, that's where you're mistaken. You trapped me into marrying you — that's all right — I'll marry you. But I'll lead my own life. And somehow — somehow I'll get a degree and be a maths teacher. And nobody, neither you nor your precious baby nor anyone else, is going to stop me! So put that in your pipe and smoke it!

He opens his book and pretends to work: but he is too agitated. MAG *covers her face and cries.*

MAN The search was continued without interruption for three days. An SOS was broadcast, and ports and airports were watched. It was reported to the police that a young couple answering to the description were seen in Liverpool and later in the Waterford area. But an investigation proved both reports to be false. Margaret Mary Enright and Joseph Michael Brennan had disappeared.

WOMAN On Wednesday, June 8, the search was called off.

Curtain

EPISODE TWO

The sun is warmer because it is early afternoon. JOE *and* MAG *have had their lunch: papers and paper cups are lying around.*

MAG *is stretched out on the ground, her head pillowed on her case; the essence of sloth. Her eyes are closed.*

JOE *is working at a calculation with total concentration.*

WOMAN   The months of June and July 1966 were the warmest and driest Ballymore has had since records have been kept. The water supply to the town had to be cut off for three hours each morning because the level of Lough Gorm dropped by almost two feet.

MAN   Beth Enright, Margaret's mother, spent the greater portion of these months in the County Psychiatric Clinic. She was visited daily by Walter, her husband, and on two occasions by Nora Brennan, Joseph's mother, who brought her grapes and magazines.

> JOE *has finished his calculations. He closes his books with a satisfied flourish.*

JOE   Maths done! They can do their damnedest now — I'm ready for them! I'll tell you something, Mag: you know when you're sitting in the exam hall and the papers have just been given out and your eye runs down the questions? Well, those are the happiest moments in my life. There's always that tiny uncertainty that maybe this time they'll come up with something that's going to throw you; but that only adds to the thrill because you know in your heart you're . . . invincible. (*He begins to put his books away: because he is on top of his work, he is in an expansive mood*) I didn't tell you; I met old Skinny Skeehan: 'I'll start you in my office, lad, as soon as your exams are over. On your mother's account I hope you're a good timekeeper and that your writing is legible.' I never looked at him right before: his eyelids are purple and his ears are all hairy. So I just said to him: 'Stick your clerkship up your legal ass and get a lawnmower at those ears of yours' — like hell. But that's what I should have said, the hungry get. (*Mentally ticking off*) About another hour to French and the same at history and I'll leave the English to tomorrow. Remember I was telling you how George Simpson got an extra degree at London University? Well, I wrote to them last night for a syllabus. Three years; that's all it takes. Joseph Brennan, Bachelor of Science. Then, by God, the world's our oyster. You asleep, Mag?

MAG (*She neither moves nor opens her eyes*) No.

JOE Nothing wrong with you, is there?

MAG No.

JOE Are you in bad form or something?

MAG No.

JOE Did I do anything, Mag?

MAG No.

JOE As long as those false pains don't come back. (*Going on gaily*) Pity we hadn't our togs. Be a great day for a swim, wouldn't it? — if we could swim!

MAG I trapped you into marrying me — that's what you said.

JOE Huh?

MAG That's what you said. Put that in your pipe and smoke it — that's what you said.

JOE Ah, come on, Mag. You're not huffing still.

MAG And you meant it, too.

JOE But you ate your lunch and all. You ate more than I did.

MAG There was hate in your eyes.

JOE I'm sorry.

MAG It's no good.

Pause. Then JOE *decides to win her round by clowning.*

JOE Mag —

MAG I'm not looking.

JOE *Mag —*

MAG No.

JOE Who's this, Mag?

MAG I'm going asleep.

JOE (*In mincing voice*) 'Tweeny — Tweeny — Tweeny —
Tweeny! Come on, Tweeny girl. Atta girl. Come on.
Come on.' /

MAG That's not one bit like Mr. O'Hara.

JOE (*In excessive nasal tones*) 'Good example is something
we should all practise, my dear people. Put one bad
apple into a barrel of good apples, and all the good
apples become corrupt.'

MAG I'm not listening.

JOE 'But put one good apple into a barrel of bad apples, and
then — and then —'

MAG You're not one bit funny.

JOE '— and then' (*rapidly*) 'devotions this evening at six
o'clock in the name of the father son holy ghost.'

MAG (*In matching tone*) Ha-men.

JOE (*East London*) 'So sorry, Joseph, but my Phil 'e's not at
'ome at present.'

MAG *suddenly giggles.*

''E's out on 'is bi-cycle on one of 'is solitary nature
rambles.'

MAG *sits up. She laughs out loud.*

'Like 'is poor dad used to. I'll tell 'im you called. Bye-
bye.'

MAG 'Ta-ta.'

JOE 'Ta-ta.'

MAG No. 'Ta-ta for now.'

JOE 'Ta-ta for now.'

MAG 'Call again soon, Joseph.'

JOE 'I like my Phil to 'ave chum boys.'

*They both howl with spontaneous, helpless laughter.
When they try to speak, they cannot finish.*

MAG Sister Pascal —

JOE Wha —

MAG Sister Pascal —

JOE — is a rascal!

MAG She says that for every five minutes you laugh, you —

JOE You what —?

MAG — you cry for ten!

> *This seems the crowning absurdity. They roll on the ground.*

JOE Oooooooh . . .!

MAG God, I'm sore!

JOE Cruel!

MAG We'll cry for weeks!

JOE Nuns — bloody nuts!

MAG Give me a handkerchief.

> *He throws her one. She wipes her eyes. They sober up — and wonder what set them off. She lights a cigarette.*

JOE What started that?

MAG I don't know.

JOE Give me (*handkerchief*). Oh, my God.

MAG Leave you weak.

JOE This whole town's nuts.

> MAG *is stretched out under the sun again. A wistful mood creeps over them now that the laughter is forgotten.*

MAG D'you think they'll get married?

JOE Who?

MAG Joan and Philip.

JOE How would I know? They're only seventeen.

MAG They say they're both going to be architects.

JOE How long does that take?

MAG Seven years. Maybe then.

> JOE *busies himself with gathering up the remains of the lunch.*

JOE Maybe then what?

MAG Maybe then they'll marry, after they qualify.

JOE Maybe. Who cares.

MAG I don't.

JOE Neither do I.

MAG Why talk about them then?

JOE You mentioned them first.

MAG You did. You imitated Mr. O'Hara and Phil's mother.

JOE Maggie, I did not mention Joan O'Hara's name. As a matter of fact, I can't stick the girl.

MAG Sister Pascal was right.

JOE What about?

MAG We *will* cry for twice the length.

JOE For God's sake, woman!

He heads off down the far side of the hill to get rid of the old papers he has gathered.

MAG (*Quickly*) Where are you going?

JOE I am going to dispose of this stuff — if I have your permission.

MAG You don't have to have my permission for anything. And I don't have to have yours either. 'Cos I'm not married to you yet, Mr. Brennan, in case you have forgotten.

JOE No, I haven't forgotten.

He disappears. She calls after him.

MAG Well, just in case you should! (*She settles back and closes her eyes resolutely*)

MAN On Tuesday, June 21, a local boy was driving his father's cows down to the edge of Lough Gorm for a drink when he saw what he described as 'bundles of clothes' floating just off the north shore. He ran home and told his mother.

WOMAN The police were informed, and Sergeant Finlay accompanied by two constables went to investigate. The 'bundles' were the bodies of Mary Margaret Enright and Joseph Michael Brennan. They were floating, fully clothed, face down, in twenty-seven inches of water.

MAN A post-mortem was held in the parochial hall at 7.00 p.m. that evening.

JOE has returned. He speaks with a dignified sincerity.

JOE Mag, there is something I never told you. And since you are going to be my wife, I don't want there to be any secrets between us. I have a post-office book. I have had it since I was ten and there is twenty-three pounds and fifteen shillings in it now. I intend spending that money on a new suit, new shoes, and an electric razor. And I'm mentioning this to you now in case you suspect I have other hidden resources. I haven't. (*He cannot maintain this tone. He continues naturally*) And I was working out our finances. The rent of the flat's two-ten. That'll leave us with about four-ten. And if I could get some private pupils, that would bring in another — say — thirty bob. We can manage fine on that, can't we? I mean, I can. What about you? (*Looks down at her*) Mag? You asleep, Mag? How the hell can you sleep when you have no work done? Maggie . . . ? (*He kneels beside her and looks into her face. He gently puts her hair away from her eyes. He straightens up as he remembers the word Caesarean*) Dictionary . . . (*He gets his own dictionary and searches for the word*) Cadet . . . cadge . . . Caesar . . . Caesarean, pertaining to Caesar or the Caesars — section — an operation by which the walls of the stomach are cut open and . . . (*Shocked and frightened*) . . . Cripes! (*Reads*) As with Julius — oh, my God! If I see you on that bike again I'll break your bloody neck! As with Julius — good God! Maggie, are you all right, Maggie? O God, that's wild, wild! Sleep, Mag; that's bound to be good for you. (*He lifts her blazer and spreads it over her*) There. God almighty! Cut open. (*Takes the blazer off*) Maybe you'll be too warm. God, I'd sit ten exams every day sooner than this! Don't say a word, Maggie; just sleep and rest! That twenty-three pound fifteen — it's for you, Maggie. And I want you to — to — to squander it just as you wish: fur coats, dresses, perfumes, make-up, all that stuff — anything in the world you want — don't even tell me what you spend it on; I don't want to know. It's yours. And curtains for the window — whatever you like. God, Mag, I never thought for a minute it was that sort of thing! (*He looks closely at her*) Mag . . . (*Whispers*) Mag, I'm not half good enough for you. I'm jealous and mean and spiteful and cruel. But I'll try to be tender to you and good to you; and that won't be hard because even when I'm not with you — just when I think of you — I go all sort of silly and I say to myself over and over again: *I'm crazy about Maggie Enright*; and so I am — crazy about you. You're a thousand times too good for me. But I'll try to be good to you; honest to God, I'll try. (*He kisses her hand and replaces it carefully across her body. Then with sudden venom*) Those Caesars were all gets! (*He takes an apple from one of the lunch bags, gets out his penknife, and peels it. As he does, he talks to* MAG *even though he knows she is asleep*) I hope it's a girl, like you; with blond hair like yours. 'Cos if it's a boy it'll be a bloody hash, like me. And every night when I come home from Skeehan's office I'll teach her maths and she'll grow up to be a prodigy. I saw a programme on TV once about an American professor who spoke to his year-old daughter in her cot in four different languages for an hour every day; and when the child began to talk she could converse in German, French, Spanish, and Italian. Imagine if my aul' fella looked down into our wee girl's cot and she shouted up to him: 'Buenos dias!' Cripes, he'd think she was giving him a tip for a horse! I hope to God it's a girl. But if it's twins I'd rather have two boys or two girls than . . . (*He glances shyly at* MAGGIE *and tails off sheepishly when he realizes he has fallen into her speech pattern*) . . . D'you hear me? That's the way married people go. They even begin to look alike. Wonder is old Skinny Skeehan married? I bet she looks like a gatepost . . . Your father, Mag, my God he's such a fine man. And your mother — I mean she's such a fine woman. I remember — oh, I was only a boy at the time — I remember seeing them walking together out the Dublin Road; and I thought they were so — you know — so dignified looking. I'd like to be like him. God, such a fine man. And so friendly to everyone. You're lucky to have parents like that . . .

My aul' fella — lifting the dole on a Friday — that's what he lives for. She laughs and calls him her man Friday; but I don't know how she can laugh at it. And to listen to him talking — cripes, you'd think he was bloody Solomon. How he can sit on his backside and watch her go out every morning with her apron wrapped in a newspaper under her arm — honest to God, I don't know how he does it. I said it to her once, you know; called him a loafer or something. And you should have seen her face! I thought she was going to hit me! 'Don't you ever — ever — say the likes of that again. You'll never be half the man he is.' Loyalty, I suppose; 'cos when you're that age, you hardly — you know — really love your husband or wife any more . . . Did I ever tell you what he does when there's no racing? He has this tin trunk under his bed; he keeps all my old school reports in it. And he sits up there in the cold and takes out the trunk and pores over all those old papers — term reports and all, away back to my primary-school days! Real nut! I know damn well when he's at it, 'cos I can hear the noise of the trunk on the lino. And once when I went into the room, he tried to stuff all the papers out of sight. Strange, too, isn't it . . . You know, we never speak at all, except maybe 'Is the tea ready?' or 'Bring in some coal.' . . . Sitting up there in that freezing attic, going over my old marks . . .

Maybe when I'm older, maybe we'll go to football matches together, like Peadar Donnelly and his aul' fella . . . I don't like football matches, but he does; and we shouldn't have to speak to each other — except going and coming back . . . Three years is no length for a degree. And I think myself I'd be a good teacher.

MAG *speaks but does not move or open her eyes. Her voice is sleepy.*

MAG What time is it?
JOE Quarter to two.

MAG Call me at half past, will you? I have a bit of revision to
do.

JOE A bit! You've done nothing!

MAG *has dropped off again.*

JOE Mag!

MAG Mm?

JOE That's all right! You go ahead and sleep! But I'm telling
you: if I die of a heart attack and leave you with a dozen
kids, you'll be damned sorry you haven't your GCE
ordinary levels!

She sits up and stares at him. He goes on defiantly.

I'm just being practical. Nowadays you're fit for nothing
unless you have an education. And you needn't stare at
me like that: any qualification is better than nothing.
You'll always get some sort of a job. Hennigan that
teaches us PT — that's all he has — is GCE. And I'm telling
you: I wouldn't give a shilling for your chances at the
moment!

MAG And the children?

JOE What children?

MAG Who's going to look after the dozen children when I'm
up at Saint Kevin's teaching physical jerks?

JOE Oh, you're very smart.

MAG And where, may I ask, did the round dozen come from
all of a sudden?

JOE Cut it out, will you? You know what I meant.

MAG Indeed I do. And if you think I'm going to spend my days
like big Bridie Brogan —

JOE Who's she supposed to be?

MAG She's married to a second cousin once removed of Joan
O'Hara's —

JOE God, I might have known! If there's anyone I hate —

MAG — *and* after her third baby the doctor told her she'd die
if she had any more; but her husband was an Irish brute
and she had a fourth báby —

JOE And she died.

40

MAG She didn't die, smartie. But she lost her sight. And then she had a fifth baby —

JOE And she died.

MAG — and she went deaf. And she couldn't walk after the sixth. And after the seventh she had to get all her teeth out —

JOE Sounds like the Rose of Tralee.

MAG And by the time she had ten —

JOE Her husband died laughing at her.

MAG — she developed pernicious micropia.

JOE Pernicious what?

MAG I'm not in the habit of repeating myself. Anyhow, she's thirty-three now and —

JOE You made that word up.

MAG I did not.

JOE You did, Maggie.

MAG I did not.

JOE Say it again, then.

MAG I told you — I'm not in —

JOE Pernicious what?

MAG You're too ignorant to have heard of it. My father came across frequent cases of it. I don't suppose your parents ever heard of it.

As soon as she has said this, she regrets it. But she cannot retract now. JOE'S *banter is suddenly ended. He is quietly furious.*

JOE Just what do you mean by that?

MAG What I say.

JOE I said: what do you mean by that remark?

MAG You heard me.

JOE You insulted my parents — deliberately.

MAG I was talking about a disease.

JOE You think they're nobody, don't you?

MAG You were mocking me.

JOE And you think your parents are somebody, don't you ?

MAG *picks a book, opens it at random, turns her back to him and begins to read.*

MAG I have revision to do.

JOE Well, let me tell you, madam, that my father may be temporarily unemployed, but he pays his bills; and *my* mother may be a charwoman but she isn't running out to the mental hospital for treatment every couple of months. And if you think the Brennans aren't swanky enough for you, then by God you shouldn't be in such a hurry to marry one of them! (*As soon as he has said this, he regrets it. But he cannot retract now*) You dragged that out of me. But it happens to be the truth. And it's better that it should come out now than *after* we're married. At least we know where we stand . . . (*His anger is dead*) Margaret? . . . Maggie? . . . (*Stiff again*) Well, it was you that started it. And if you're going into another of your huffs, I swear to you I'm not going to be the first to speak this time.

> *He picks a book, opens it at random, turns his back to her, and begins to read.*

WOMAN At the post-mortem on the evening of June 21 evidence of identification was given by Walter Enright. He said that the body recovered from Lough Gorm was the body of his daughter, Margaret Mary Enright.

MAN Michael Brennan identified the male body as that of his son, Joseph Michael Brennan.

WOMAN Doctor Watson said that he examined the bodies of both the deceased. There were no marks of violence on either, he said. And in his opinion — which, he submitted, was given after a hasty examination — death in both cases was due to asphyxiation.

MAN Mr. Skeehan, the coroner, asked was there any evidence as to how both deceased fell into the water. Sergeant Finlay replied that there was no evidence.

WOMAN A verdict in accordance with the medical evidence was returned. Mr. Skeehan and Sergeant Finlay expressed their grief and the grief of the community to the parents. And it was agreed that the inquest should be held as soon as possible because the coroner took his annual vacation in the month of July.

JOE *looks up from his book and surveys the countryside with studied intelligence. When he speaks he tries to sound as matter-of-fact as possible — as if he were continuing a conversation: but his voice is strained.*

JOE We're about 450 feet above sea level here; isn't that interesting? (*Pause*) And all that area out there was covered with fir trees once. (*Pause*) Willie O'Rourke did a survey of the whole area for his geography practical last term and he found out all sorts of fascinating things. (*Pause*) The average rainfall in Ballymore is 17.4 percent above the county average and 23.9 percent above the national average. (*Pause*) That's because we get a lot of rain here. (*Quoting*) And the moist climate determines the type and extent of our husbandry: we are low in milk cattle and high in mountain sheep. (*Pause*) And since a ring of hills cuts us off from other community centres we are traditionally inclined to be independent and self-supporting — or so he claims. (*Pause*) It's an interesting hypothesis. (*Pause*) Busy? (*No answer. Formally*) I'm sorry for losing my temper. (*Opens another book*) If you have anything to say to me, you'll find me here. (*No answer. He looks at her*) You're crying? . . . Mag? . . . (*Still no answer. He rises and stands behind her*) What the hell are you crying about, Mag? . . . Mag . . . (*He goes in front of her. She turns her back to him*) I said I'm sorry. What more can I do . . . ? (*Pause*) It's going to be just great if you're going to spend your life weeping all the time! (*He casts around wretchedly for something to entertain her. Decides on mimicry. As* MRS. MORAN) 'Well, I mean to say — smoking at 'is age! I just says to 'im, "Phil," I says, "if your poor daddy was alive, 'e'd be so vexed," I says. "Ta-ta for now, Joe. Ta-ta for now."'(*No response from* MAG. *As* KERRIGAN) 'What about that for a bit of beef, eh? Bang. Best flat in town, lad. I could have let it a dozen times over. Bang. Bang. Bang.' (*No response*) Mag . . . Mag, is it true that in bed at night the nuns wear their bloomers over their heads to keep them warm? (*No response. Sings*)

'So I gave her kisses one, kisses one;
So I gave her kisses one, kisses one;
So I gave her kisses one — now the fun has just begun
So I settled down to give her kisses more.'
(*Says*) I'd be great on TV, wouldn't I? (*No response*)
When Father Kelly sent for me last Friday fortnight, I
knew I was done for, and I pretended I was so frightened
I had a stammer — did I tell you that part of it?

(*Pompous*) 'You know, of course, Brennan, that we
are going to expel you.'

(*Abject*) 'Yes, F-f-f-father.'

(*Pompus*) 'Because of your mother's pleadings on
your behalf, however, we have decided to allow you to
return to sit for your examinations. But in the meantime
I must insist that you remove all your belongings from
the college and that you don't set foot within the grounds
until the morning of the first examination.'

(*Abject*) 'T-t-t-thank you, Father.'

(*Pompous*) 'I will not talk again about the dishonour
you have brought to your school, your family, and
yourself. And I trust you have made your peace with
God. Goodbye, Brennan.'

(*Abject*) 'Goodbye, Father.'

(*Pompous*) 'Incidentally, Brennan, when did you
develop the stammer?'

(*Abject*) 'W-w-w-when Maggie told me she was in
trouble, Father.'

> MAG *began chuckling silently — and unnoticed by* JOE
> *— at the beginning of this interview. Now she can
> contain her laughter no longer. At the last line she
> screams her delight and throws herself at him, and they
> roll on the ground.*

MAG God forgive you!
JOE Stop! Stop! God's truth —
MAG God forgive you! Mocking's catching!
JOE Come on — quit the fooling.
MAG I'll give you a stammer. (*She tosses his hair and tickles
him*)

44

JOE Mag — please — sorry — please — oooooh —
MAG I'll stammer you —
JOE You're hurting my —
MAG That'll teach you!
JOE You've ripped off a button —
MAG You're a right-looking sketch!

Exhausted after the wrestling, they sit staring at one another. Suddenly he throws his arms around her and kisses her. As he does:

MAN On Saturday, June 25, at 11.00 a.m. an inquest was held.
WOMAN After various witnesses had given evidence about the movements of the deceased on the morning of Saturday, June 4, Doctor Watson said that the State Pathologist's report bore out his initial opinion — that death was due to asphyxiation as a result of drowning.
MAN There was no evidence as to how the deceased got into the water. William Anthony Clerkin's boat was perfectly sound.
WOMAN Sergeant Finlay stated that the temperature on that afternoon was 77 degrees. And there was no wind.
MAN An open verdict was returned.
WOMAN On the following Sunday, June 5, at 12 noon, a solemn requiem mass was said by Father Kelly, president of Saint Kevin's, and a short panegyric was preached by him. The mass was attended by a large turn-out of the townspeople and also by pupils of the Convent of Mercy and Saint Kevin's.
MAN The bodies were buried in separate graves in the local cemetery, each in the family plot.

JOE and MAG are now sitting with their arms around one another, looking down over the town. The boisterousness is all over; the mood is calm, content, replete. MAG lights a cigarette.

JOE This day three weeks.
MAG Mrs. Joseph Brennan.
JOE As long as you're not Big Bridie Brogan.

45

MAG Who?

JOE The one who died of pernicious something or other.

MAG I made it all up.

JOE Thought you did.

MAG The flat'll be lovely and cozy at night. But you'll have to stick a bit of cardboard under the table to keep it steady. And all the junk'll have to be thrown into the spare room.

JOE What junk?

MAG Your books and things and all that.

JOE The slide rule cost me thirty-seven and sixpence — It's staying in the kitchen. And you agreed that the dog sleeps inside.

MAG When do we get him?

JOE He's not pupped yet. I was only promised him.

MAG Maybe he'll be a she.

JOE It's a dog I'm promised — the pick of the litter.

MAG We'll call him . . . Austin!

JOE For God's sake —

MAG Austin's his name. Or else he sleeps out.

JOE Never heard of a bull terrier called that.

MAG And in the daytime he can sit at the door and guard the pram. Look —

JOE Where?

MAG The line of boarders.

JOE What are they up to now?

MAG Going to the chapel for a visit.

JOE (*Counting*) 14, 16, 18, 20 —

MAG It seems so remote — so long ago . . .

JOE — 26, 28, 30, 32 —

MAG And at home last week, every time I heard the convent bell, I cried: I felt so lost. I would have given anything to be part of them — to be in the middle of them.

JOE And three nuns.

MAG We were so safe . . . we had so much fun . . .

JOE Mm?

MAG But now I wouldn't go back for the world. I'm a woman at seventeen, and I wouldn't be a schoolgirl again, not for all the world.

JOE I suppose I'm a man, too.

MAG Would you go back?

JOE Where?

MAG To Saint Kevin's — to being a schoolboy?

JOE I never think of things like that.

MAG But if you could — if you had a chance.

JOE I like studying, Mag.

MAG Then you'd prefer to go back.

JOE No. Not there. I'm finished with all that.

MAG Then you wouldn't want to go back?

JOE Not to Saint Kevin's. No.

MAG Good.

JOE Know something, Mag?

MAG Mm?

JOE I think I should forget about studying and London University and all that.

MAG If that's what you want.

JOE It's maybe not what I want. But that's the way things have turned out. A married man with a family has more important things to occupy his mind besides bloody books.

She gives him a brief squeeze. But she has not heard what he has said. Pause.

Ballymore.

MAG Home.

JOE See the sun glinting on the headstones beside the chapel.

MAG Some day we'll be buried together.

JOE You're great company.

MAG I can't wait for the future, Joe.

JOE What's that supposed to mean?

MAGGIE suddenly leaps to her feet. Her face is animated, her movements quick and vital, her voice ringing.

MAG The past's over! And I hate this waiting time! I want the future to happen — I want to be in it — I want to be in it with you!

JOE You've got sunstroke.

She throws her belongings into her case.

MAG Come on, Joe! Let's begin the future now!

Not comprehending, but infected by her mood, he gets to his feet.

JOE You're nuts.

MAG Where'll we go? What'll we do? Let's do something crazy!

JOE Mad as a hatter.

MAG The lake! We'll dance on every island! We'll stay out all night and sing and shout at the moon! (JOE *does a wolf howl up at the sky*) Come on, Joe! While the sun's still hot!

JOE O mad hot sun, thou breath of summer's being!

MAG Away to the farthest island.

JOE We've no boat.

MAG We'll take one.

JOE And get arrested.

MAG Coward. Then I'll take one.

JOE I'll visit you in jail.

MAG Quick! Quick!

JOE throws his books into his bag.

JOE Hold on there.

MAG Give me your hand. We'll run down the hill.

JOE You'll get those pains again.

MAG Your hand.

JOE You're not going to run down there.

MAG Come on! Come on! Come on!

JOE Have sense, Mag —

She catches his hand and begins to run.

MAG We're away!

JOE Easy — easy —

MAG Wheeeeeeeee —

JOE Aaaaaaaaah —

They run down the hill, hand in hand. At the bottom
JOE *takes her bicycle. Their voices fade slowly. Pause.*
Then:

MAN Beth Enright's health has improved greatly. She has not
had a relapse for almost seven months. And every
evening, if the weather is good, Walter and she go for a
walk together out the length of Whelan's Brae.
WOMAN Mick Brennan never mentions his son's name. After the
funeral he took a tin trunk out to the waste ground
behind Railway Terrace and burned all the contents.
Nora Brennan has had to limit the amount of work she
does because her varicose veins turned septic and
Doctor Watson ordered her to rest. She now works on
afternoons only.
MAN In the past eight months the population of Ballymore has
risen from 13,527 to 13,569.
WOMAN Life there goes on as usual.
MAN As if nothing had ever happened.

The MAN *and* WOMAN *close their texts, stand up, and*
exit, one left, one right.

Losers

The stage is divided into three equal areas: the portion right is the back yard of a working-class terrace house; the centre portion is the kitchen/living room; the area left is the bedroom (left and right from the point of view of the audience). There should be no attempts at a realistic division of the stage areas, no dividing walls, no detailed furnishings: frames will indicate doors, etc., etc.

The back yard is suggested by a dustbin and by two high stone walls (one back stage and one right). It is a grey, grimy, gloomy, sunless place.

The kitchen is furnished with a table and a few chairs, and with a disproportionately large horsehair black couch. The couch sits along the imaginary wall between the kitchen and the back yard. There are three doors leading out of the kitchen: one to the yard, one to the scullery (unseen) and one to the hall/stairs (unseen).

The bedroom area is raised on a shallow platform which is approached by two steps (because this room is supposed to be directly above the kitchen). It is furnished with a big iron double bed, a chest of drawers (the 'altar'), and a few chairs. Except where indicated, the bedroom will be hidden from the audience by a large draft screen.

TIME: *The present in Ireland.*

When the curtain rises, ANDY TRACEY *is sitting upright and motionless on a kitchen chair in the back yard. He is staring fixedly through a pair of binoculars at the grey stone wall, which is only a few yards from where he is sitting. It becomes obvious that he is watching nothing: there is nothing to watch, and when he becomes aware of the audience, he lowers the glasses slowly, looks at the audience, glances cautiously over his shoulder at the kitchen to make sure that no one in the house overhears him, and then speaks directly and confidentially down to the auditorium.*

He is a man of fifty, a joiner by trade, heavily built. His workmates look on him as a solid, decent, reliable, slightly dull man. Because his

*mind is simple, direct, unsubtle, he is unaware of the humour in a lot
of the things that he says.*

ANDY I'll tell you something: I see damn-all through these
things. Well, I mean, there's damn-all to see in a back
yard. Now and again maybe a sparrow or something
like that lands on top of the wall there but it's so close
it's only a blur. Anyway, most of the time I sit with my
eyes closed. And Hanna — she probably knows I do
'cos she's no dozer; but once I come out here — I'll say
that for her — she leaves me alone. A gesture I make,
and she — you know — she respects it. Maybe because
her aul' fella used to do the same thing; for that's where
I learned the dodge. As a matter of fact, these are his
glasses. And this is where he was found dead, the poor
bugger, just three years ago, slumped in a chair out
here, and him all happed up in his cap and his top coat
and his muffler and his woollen gloves. Wait — I'm
telling you a lie. Four years ago — aye — that's more
like it, 'cos he passed away that January Hanna and me
started going, and we won't be married four years until
next summer. Not that I knew the man, beyond
bidding him the time of day there. Maybe he'd be
inside in the kitchen, there or more likely sitting out
here, and I'd say to him, 'Hello there, Mr. Wilson' —
you know the way, when you're going with a woman,
you try to be affable to her aul' fella — and he'd say,
'Oh, hello there, Andy,' or something like that back.
But you know yourself, a man that's looking through
binoculars, you don't like interrupting him. Civil wee
man he was, too. Fifty years a stoker out in the general
hospital. And a funny thing — one of the male nurses
out there was telling me — all his life he stuck to the
night shift: worked all night and slept all day, up there
in that room above the kitchen. Peculiar, eh? All his
life. Never saw the wife except maybe for a couple of
hours in the evening. Never saw Hanna, the daughter,
except at the weekends. Funny, eh? And yet by all
accounts the civilest and decentest wee man you could
meet. Funny, too. And the way things turn out in life;

when the mother-in-law found him out here about seven o'clock that evening, she got such a bloody fright that she collapsed and took to the bed for good and hasn't risen since, not even the morning we got married. The heart. But that's another story. Anyway, Hanna and me, as I say, we were only started going at the time; and then with the aul' fella dying and the aul' woman taking to the bed, like we couldn't go out to the pictures nor dances nor nothing like any other couple; so I started coming here every evening. And this is where we done our courting, in there, on the couch. (*Chuckles briefly*) By God, we were lively enough, too. Eh? I mean to say, people think that when you're . . . well, when you're over the forty mark, that you're passified. But aul' Hanna, by God, I'll say that for her, she was keen as a terrier in those days. (*Chuckles at the memory*) If that couch could write a book — Shakespeare, how are you! (*He rises from the chair*) Every evening, after I'd leave the workshop, I'd go home to my own place at Riverview and wash myself down and make a sup of tea and put on the good suit and call in at Boyce's paper shop and get a quarter of clove rock — that's the kind she liked — and come on over here and there she'd be, waiting for me, in a grey skirt and a blue jumper, and when she'd open the door to me, honest to God the aul' legs would damn near buckle under me.

HANNA *comes into the kitchen from upstairs. She is dressed in a grey skirt and blue jumper.* ANDY *walks through the invisible walls, through the hall, and taps on the kitchen door.*
HANNA *is in her late forties. She works in a local shirt factory, lives alone with her invalided mother, and until* ANDY *came on the scene has not been out with a man for over twenty years. And this sudden injection of romance into a life that seemed to be rigidly and permanently patterned has transformed a very plain spinster into an almost attractive woman. With* ANDY *she is warm: with her mother she reverts to waspishness.*

Because neither ANDY *nor* HANNA *is young, there is a curious and slightly dated diffidence between them. And yet, when they begin courting, it is* HANNA *who takes the initiative and caresses him with a vigour and concentration that almost embarrass him.*

ANDY   Well, Hanna.

HANNA   Hello, Andy.

ANDY   Not a bad evening.

HANNA   There's a cold wind, though.

ANDY   It's sharp — sharp.

HANNA   But it's nice all the same.

ANDY   Oh, very nice — very fresh. (*Pause*) Nothing startling at the factory?

HANNA   Not a thing. Working away.

ANDY   Suppose so.

HANNA   Cutting out shirt collars this week. And you?

ANDY   Still at the furniture for the new hotel. Going to cost a fortune, yon place.

HANNA   I'll bet you.

ANDY   Only the very best of stuff going into it: maple and pine and mahogany. Lovely to work with.

HANNA   D'you see that now.

ANDY   Lovely.

Pause. Then ANDY *produces the small bag of sweets from his pocket.*

ANDY   Here. Catch. (*He throws them to her*)

HANNA   Oh, Andy . . .

ANDY   They don't even ask me in the shop any more. They just say, 'Quarter pound of clove rock, Mr. Tracey. Right you are.'

HANNA   You have me spoiled.

ANDY   How's the mother?

HANNA   (*Sharply*) Living. And praying.

ANDY   Terrible sore thing, the heart, all the same.

HANNA   I come home from my work beat out and before I get a bite in my mouth she says, 'Run out like a good child and get us a sprig of fresh flowers for Saint Philomena's

altar.'
ANDY Did you go?

HANNA points to the flowers wrapped in paper lying on the kitchen table.

HANNA But she can wait for them.
ANDY She'll miss you when you leave, Hanna.
HANNA Hasn't she Cissy Cassidy next door? And if she hadn't a slavey like me to wait hand and foot on her, her heart mightn't be just as fluttery! (*From behind the screen comes the sound of a bell — not a tinkling little bell, but a huge brass bell with a long wooden handle*) We're early at it the night! There's the paper. Have a look at it.

With a bad grace she goes to answer the summons. As she is about to exit:

ANDY The flowers.

She grabs them, grimaces, and leaves. ANDY calls after her:

Tell Saint Philomena I was asking for her!

He chuckles at HANNA's bad humour. Then he comes down stage and addresses the audience.

That bloody bell! And nine times out of ten, you know, she didn't want a damn thing: Who's at the door? Is the fire safe? Did the Angelus ring? Is it time for the Rosary? Any excuse at all to keep Hanna on the hop, and at the same time making damn sure we weren't going to enjoy ourselves. But we got cute. You see, every sound down here carries straight up to her room; and we discovered that it was the long silences made her suspicious. That's the way with a lot of pious aul' women — they have wild dirty imaginations. And as soon as there was a silence down here, she thought we were up to something and reached for the bloody bell. But if there was the sound of plenty of chatting down here, she seldom bothered you. But I mean to say, if you're courting a woman there, you can't keep yapping about the weather all night. And it was the brave Hanna that hit on the poetry idea. Whenever we started the courting, she made me recite the poetry — you know there, just to make a bit of a noise. And the only poetry I ever learned at school was a thing called *Elegy Written in a Country Churchyard* by Thomas Gray, 1716 to 1771, if you ever heard tell of it. And I used to recite that over and over again. And Hanna, she would throw an odd word in there to make it sound natural. And, by God, we'd hammer away at it until we'd stop for breath or for a sup of tea or something; or else we'd get carried away and forget the aul' woman altogether — and then the bloody bell would go and the session would be destroyed. But they were good times . . . Funny thing about that poem, too: it had thirty-two verses, and as long as I could bull straight at it — you know, without thinking what I was saying — I could rattle it off like a man. But stop me in the middle of it or let me think of what I was saying, and I had to go right back to the beginning and start all over again. Christ, they were rare times, too . . .

HANNA *returns.*

ANDY Well?

HANNA 'Is that Andrew I hear?' 'No,' says I, 'it's Jack the Ripper.'

ANDY And how's Saint Philomena?

HANNA You can laugh. 'The pair of you'll be up later for the Rosary, won't you?'

ANDY (*Mock devotion*) With the help of God.

HANNA One of these days I'll do something desperate.

She sits dispiritedly beside him on the couch. He wants to say something tender and consoling to her but feels he is past the age for effusive, extravagant language.

ANDY You're looking nice, Hanna.
HANNA It's the jumper.

> *Pause. Then he takes her hand in his and strokes it. She raises his hand to her lips and kisses it gently again and again. He puts his arm round her shoulder. They sit like this for some time.*

We'd better keep talking.
ANDY There's a nice smell of you.
HANNA Soap.
ANDY Nice soap.
HANNA (*Dreamily*) Her bloody ear'll be twitching like a rabbit.
ANDY Hanna . . .

> *Pause. They speak the next eight lines as if they were in a trance.*

HANNA Say something, Andy.
ANDY I don't want to.
HANNA Please, Andy. She'll know.
ANDY I don't give a damn.
HANNA Andy . . .
ANDY Nice . . .
HANNA Please, Andy . . .
ANDY Very nice . . .

> *Very suddenly, almost violently,* HANNA *flings herself on him so that he falls back, and she buries her face in his neck and kisses and caresses him with astonishing passion. He is momentarily at a loss. But this has happened before, many times, and he knows that this is his cue to begin his poem. His recitation is strained and too high and too loud — like a child in school memorizing meaningless facts. Throughout his recital, they court feverishly.*

ANDY 'The curfew tolls the knell of parting day,

The lowing herd wind slowly o'er the lea,
        The plowman homeward plods his weary way,
        And leaves the world to darkness and to me.
        Now fades the glimmering landscape on the sight —'
HANNA (*To ceiling*) It's a small world, isn't it?
 ANDY 'Now fades the glimmering landscape on the sight,
        And all the air a solemn stillness holds,
        Save where the beetle wheels his droning flight,
        And drowsy tinklings lull the distant folds —'
        Oh, God, Hanna —
HANNA Just imagine. Fancy that. Keep going, man.
 ANDY 'Save that from yonder ivy-mantled tow'r
        The moping owl does to the moon complain
        Of such as, wand'ring near her secret bow'r,
        Molest her ancient solitary reign.'
HANNA Andy — Andy —
 ANDY 'Beneath those rugged elms, that yew-tree's shade —'

        HANNA *groans voluptuously.*

 ANDY Steady on — steady on — say something —
HANNA Mm?
 ANDY She'll be listening to —
HANNA I don't give a damn.
 ANDY (*To ceiling*) Fine. Yes, indeed. Imagine that. Where in
        the name of God was I?
HANNA 'That yew-tree's shade —'
 ANDY What, where?
HANNA 'Beneath those rugged elms.'
 ANDY Oh. 'Beneath those rugged elms, that yew-tree's
        shade,
        Where heaves the turf in many a mould'ring heap,
        Each in his narrow cell for ever laid,
        The rude Forefathers of the hamlet sleep.'
        Speak, woman!

        She kisses him on the mouth.

 ANDY Say something!
HANNA Kiss me.

ANDY For God's sake, woman —
HANNA Andy, kiss me.

> *He kisses her. They forget everything. The clanging of the bell shatters the silence — and* HANNA *breaks away roughly from him, jumps to her feet, and is almost trembling with fury. Her jumper and skirt are twisted.*

HANNA Bitch! The aul' bitch!
ANDY Sure you're only after leaving her! What the hell can she want?
HANNA Stuffed!
ANDY Your jumper.
HANNA Agh! My . . .!

> *She pulls the jumper right up and then pulls it back into place.* ANDY *laughs at her anger.*

ANDY Go on — go on — go on. A girl's best friend is her mother.
HANNA Shut up, will you.

> *She adjusts her skirt and brushes back her hair and charges out of the room.* ANDY *looks after her and smiles contentedly. Then he addresses the audience.*

ANDY By God, she had spunk in those days, eh? Suited her, too: gave her face a bit of colour and made her eyes dance. But whatever it was that happened to her — well, I mean to say, I think I know what happened . . . But, like, to see a woman that had plenty of spark in her at one time and then to see her turn before your very eyes into a younger image of her mother, by God it's strange, I tell you, very peculiar. . .

But I was going to tell you about the aul' woman and the altar and the Rosary and Saint Philomena and Father Peyton and all that caper. The routine was this. At the stroke of ten every night wee Cissy Cassidy — her and the aul' woman's well met; two lisping Lizzies

— she came down and asked Hanna and me to go up for the nightly Rosary. Fair enough. Why not? And there's the aul' woman lying in the bed, smiling like an angel, and there, smiling back at her from the top of a chest of drawers, is this big statue of Saint Philomena. And you know, you got this feeling, with the flowers and the candles lit and with all the smirking and smiling and nodding and winking, you got the feeling by God that you were up to the neck in some sort of a deep plot or other. Like I knew damn well what the aul' woman was up to: if she couldn't break it up between Hanna and me, at least she was going to make damn sure that I wasn't going to take Hanna away from her. And *she* knew that *I* knew what she was up to with her wee sermons about Father Peyton and all the stuff about the family that prays together stays together. And there was the pair of us, watching and smiling, each of us knowing that the other knew, and none of us giving away anything. By God, it was strange. Eh? 'Cos she thought that every time I got down on my knees in that bedroom to join in the Rosary I was cutting my own throat. But because I knew what she was up to, I was safe . . . or at least I thought I was. She's crafty, that aul' woman. You've got to hand it to her. By God she's crafty.

He goes upstage and casually lifts the newspaper to glance over it. HANNA *enters on her way through to the scullery. She is carrying her mother's soiled tray.*

HANNA Look at — the invalid tray! Not a crumb on it! Six rounds of a sliced-pan and a boiled egg! Thanks be to God she gets no fresh air or she'd eat up the town! (*Knock at the front door*) That'll be prissy Cissy.

She goes off to the scullery. ANDY *goes to open the door.* CISSY *and* ANDY *come back to the kitchen briefly before* CISSY *goes upstairs.*
CISSY *is a small, frail wisp of a woman in her late sixties. She lives next door, is a daily visitor, and*

because of the close friendship between herself and
MRS WILSON *she has a proprietary air in the house.*
A lifetime spent lisping pious platitudes has robbed
them of all meaning. The sickly piousity she exudes is
patently false.

ANDY Hello, Cissy.

CISSY Good night, Andrew. You're not alone, are you?

ANDY Hanna's inside. How's things, Cissy?

CISSY Struggling away, Andrew, thanks be to God. Sure as long as we have our health.

ANDY That's it, Cissy.

CISSY Thanks be to God, indeed. I'll go on up then, Andrew.

ANDY Right — right.

CISSY You'll be up later for the prayers?

ANDY Aye.

CISSY Thanks be to God.

> HANNA *enters from the scullery. She is abrupt with*
> CISSY.

Hello, Hanna. How's Mammy tonight?

HANNA As ever.

CISSY Sure that's grand.

ANDY (*Winking at* HANNA) Thanks be to God.

CISSY Just, Andrew — thanks be to God. Well . . . I'll see you both at ten.

ANDY Joyful mysteries tonight, Cissy, isn't it?

CISSY Thursday — so it is! Oh, you're coming closer and closer to us, Andrew Tracey!

> *She leaves.* ANDY *laughs.*

HANNA Sweet wee wasp!

> HANNA *flops down on the couch.* ANDY *sits beside her.*
> *He sees she is in bad form and tries to coax her out of*
> *it.*

ANDY Tired?

HANNA   Done out.

ANDY   D'you think was Cissy ever courted?

HANNA   Who cares?

ANDY   Imagine a man putting a hand on her knee. 'Thanks be to God, mister.' (*She does not laugh*) You're in bad aul' form, Hanna.

He puts his arm round her. She jumps to her feet.

HANNA   Not now.

ANDY   What's wrong? Is there something the matter?

HANNA   Sick — sick — sick — sick of the whole thing; that's what's the matter! I can't stand it much longer!

ANDY   Take a clove rock, Hanna.

HANNA   What in the name of God are we going to do?

ANDY   I've asked you half a dozen times to —

HANNA   It's her I'm talking about! Her up there! What do we do with her?

ANDY   When we're married she can come with us to River-view. I've said that all —

HANNA   Never! Never! The day I get married I'm getting shot of her for good!

ANDY spreads his hands: 'What can I reply to that,' the gesture says.

And no matter what you say now, you know fine well you don't want her hanging round your neck either.

ANDY   I hear they took old Maggie Donaldson into Saint Patrick's.

HANNA   She's not sick enough for hospital. And they've no spare beds for cranks.

ANDY   The Nazareth nuns! Let her sell this place and go into the Nazareth House with the money.

HANNA   She wouldn't go to them above all people.

ANDY   What else is there?

HANNA   I don't know, Andy. Honest to God, I just don't know.

Pause, and it dawns on ANDY that an offer is expected from him. He reacts strongly to the unspoken idea.

ANDY   Well, damnit all, you don't expect me to come in here, do you? I mean to say, I have a place and all of my own, ready and furnished and everything! And leaping sky-high every time you hear a bloody bell isn't my idea of married bliss! My God, you don't expect that of me, do you? Well, do you?

HANNA   Bitch! That's what she is — an aul' bitch!

ANDY   We're getting no younger, Hanna, you know.

HANNA   Tomorrow — I'll tell her tomorrow that we're going to clear out and she can damn well forage for herself!

ANDY   You'll like it over at Riverview. It's — it's — (*He sees that she is crying*) Hanna, Hanna — aw, God, you're not away crying, are you —

He puts his arm round her and leads her to the couch. They sit. She blows her nose while he tries to console her.

Come on, come on, there's no need for that. You know I can't stand seeing you crying. And you know I'd do anything to make you happy. We'll solve it some way or other. Don't you worry about it — we'll get some solution to it all.

HANNA   No, we won't.

ANDY   I'm telling you we will.

HANNA   No, no. And only this morning I found myself singing at my work. And sure I can't even sing in tune.

ANDY   I could listen to you all day.

HANNA   But sure nobody goes through life singing all the time.

ANDY   We will, Hanna.

Very suddenly, almost violently — exactly as before — HANNA flings herself on him and smothers him with kisses. And as before, he is taken unawares. Then he responds. But after a few seconds he realizes that they are being silent and he launches into his poem.

'The curfew tolls the knell of parting day,
  The lowing herd wind slowly o'er the lea,
  The plowman homeward plods his weary way,

And leaves the world to darkness and to me.'
Hanna . . . !

She does not hear him. Pause. Then he goes on.

'Now fades the glimmering landscape on the sight,
    And all the air a solemn stillness holds,
    Save where the beetle wheels his droning flight,
    And drowsy tinklings lull the distant folds.'
Say something, woman!

HANNA A loaf of bread costs one and threepence ha'penny and a pound of tea six and eight pence.

ANDY 'Full many a gem of purest ray serene
The dark unfathom'd caves of ocean bear:
E'en from the tomb the voice of Nature cries —'
I've bucked it!

HANNA 'Can storied urn or animated bust —'

ANDY What — what — what is it?

HANNA 'Back to its mansion call the fleeting breath.'

ANDY '. . . call the fleeting breath?
Can Honour's voice provoke the silent dust,
Or Flatt'ry soothe the dull cold ear of death?
Perhaps in this neglected spot is laid
Some heart once pregnant with celestial fire;
Hands, that the rod of empire might have swayed . . .'

But he fades out because he can no longer resist the barrage of her passion. Their mouths meet. A long kiss. Silence. Then — the bell. HANNA *springs to her feet. This time* ANDY *is angry too.*

HANNA Christ!

ANDY For God's sake!

HANNA Bitch! Bitch! Bitch! Bitch! Bitch!

ANDY It's your fault! You make no attempt at all.

HANNA I don't know no poems!

ANDY Well . . . bloody shopping lists . . . multiplication tables . . . anything! (*Again the bell*) What the hell can she want? Isn't Cissy with her?

HANNA (*Evenly*) One of these days I'm going to strangle that woman . . . with her Rosary beads.

She marches off. ANDY *grabs a paper and tries to read it. We now see* HANNA *enter the bedroom and we hear* MRS WILSON'S *voice.*

MRS WILSON We're going to say the Rosary a bit earlier tonight, dear. Cissy has a bit of a headache.

HANNA *removes the screen and puts it to the side of the set. In the large iron bed, propped up against the pillows, lies* MRS WILSON. *Like* CISSY, *she is a tiny woman, with a sweet, patient, invalid's smile. Her voice is soft and commanding. Her silver hair is drawn back from her face and tied with a blue ribbon behind her head. She looks angelic.*
CISSY, *her understudy, is sitting beside her, watching her with devotion.*
Directly facing MRS WILSON *is a chest of drawers, on which are a white cloth, two candles, a large statue of a saint, and a vase of flowers — a miniature altar.* MRS WILSON *frequently nods and smiles to the statue and mouths 'Thank you, thank you.'* HANNA *clumps around the room, doing her chores with an ungracious vigour and with obvious ill-will.*

HANNA Whatever suits Cissy suits me!

CISSY She's looking lovely tonight, Hanna, isn't she? It must be the good care you're taking of her.

MRS WILSON I'm blessed, Cissy dear, and I know it. A good daughter is a gift of God. (*To the statue*) Thank you. (*To* HANNA *who is fixing the bed clothes too robustly*) That's fine, dear, thank you. Just fine.

HANNA Pillows.

MRS WILSON What's that, dear?

HANNA D'you want me to beat up the pillows?

MRS WILSON No, I'm grand. A wee bit of discomfort's good for me.

CISSY Invalids is all saints — that's what I say.

MRS WILSON Here's the matches, dear.

HANNA *goes and lights the candles.*

MRS WILSON Cissy, could I trouble you to give Andrew a call?
CISSY Pleasure.
MRS WILSON (*To* HANNA) And maybe you'd be good enough to move Saint Philomena round a wee bit so that she's facing me . . . just a little to the left . . . so that we're looking at each other . . . That's it. Lovely. Thank you, dear.
CISSY (*Off and unseen*) Andrew!
MRS WILSON God be praised a thousand times. Saint Vibiana, Virgin and Martyr, protect us. Saint Hyacintha de Mariscottis, look after us this day and this night.
CISSY (*Off*) The Rosary!
ANDY (*Off*) Coming.
MRS WILSON (*To* HANNA) And my jewels, dear.
HANNA What are you saying?
MRS WILSON Could you hand me my beads, please? (HANNA *does this*) God bless you. Another day is nearly o'er. A journey closer to the heavenly shore.

Enter CISSY.

CISSY He's coming. Thanks be to God.
MRS WILSON Amen to that. Poor Hanna's run off her feet, isn't she?
CISSY A labour of love.

ANDY *enters. He tries to be brisk and matter-of-fact in this cloying feminine atmosphere.*

MRS WILSON Ah, Andrew!
ANDY How are you tonight, Mrs. Wilson?
MRS WILSON Grand, Andrew, thanks. I have Saint Philomena during the day and I have you all at night.
ANDY Very nice.
MRS WILSON Are you going to join us in the prayers?
HANNA Didn't you send down for him!
MRS WILSON Thank you, Andrew. As Father Peyton says: the family that prays together stays together.
HANNA Get started.

66

MRS WILSON And Father Peyton is right, isn't he, Andrew?

ANDY Right, Mrs. Wilson.

MRS WILSON If you only knew the consolation it is for me to have you all kneeling round my bed.

CISSY It's what you deserve.

MRS WILSON Thank you, Saint Philomena. Thank you.

HANNA Who's giving it out?

MRS WILSON Aren't the flowers pretty, Andrew?

ANDY Very nice.

MRS WILSON Hanna got them for me. But then — why wouldn't she? Didn't she take the name Philomena for her confirmation.

HANNA Lookat — are we going to say the prayers or are we not?

CISSY Hanna dear, you're talking to a sick woman.

MRS WILSON (*Laying a restraining hand on* CISSY) She's tired, Cissy. I know. I don't mind. Maybe you'd give it out tonight, Andrew, would you?

ANDY I — I — I —

HANNA He will not, then. I will.

> MRS WILSON *mouths her thanks to the statue.* HANNA *begins at top speed.*

HANNA In the name of the Father and of the Son and of the Holy Ghost. We fly to thy protection, O holy mother of God. Despise not our prayers in our necessity, but deliver us from all dangers, O glorious and ever blessed virgin. Thou O Lord will open my lips.

OTHERS And my tongue shall announce thy praise.

HANNA Incline unto my aid, O God.

OTHERS O Lord, make haste to help me.

HANNA Glory be to the Father and to the Son and to the Holy Ghost.

OTHERS As it was in the beginning, is now, and ever shall be, world without end, Amen.

> *They are all on their knees around the bed, facing the altar now. While the prayers continue,* ANDY *gets to his feet and places the screen in its opening position —*

that is, completely hiding the bedroom. He then goes behind the screen to continue the Rosary.
The lights come down slowly and the prayers fade.
Total black for about a minute.

When the lights go up, ANDY *is sitting as we first saw him, in the back yard, with his binoculars. He leaves down the binoculars, glances cautiously over his shoulder at the kitchen to make sure that no one in the house overhears him, and then speaks to the audience.*

ANDY   The big mistake I made was to come back here after the honeymoon — *even* for the couple of weeks that it was supposed to be at the beginning. I should have put the foot down then. But, like, everything happened so sudden. One bright morning the firm turns round and says 'All the single men in the joinery room are being sent to Belfast on a contract job.' So there was nothing for it, like, but to get married. And that's what we done. And then when we got back from the three days in Dublin, there's the damn painters still hashing about in Riverview, and the aul' woman has a bit of 'flu, and Hanna's kind of worried about her, and damnit, between one thing and another we find ourselves back here. But it was to have been only for a couple of weeks — that was the arrangement — aw, no, there was no doubt about that. Two weeks, she said. And a funny thing, you know, looking back on it, there was a change in the tune even then. No, not so much with the aul' woman — she's too crafty — Christ, you've got to hand it to the aul' woman — but with Hanna. Like, you know, before we got married, she was full of fight, there: let the aul' woman step out of line or say something sharp to me and by God she jumped at her like a cock at a gooseberry. But somehow the spirit seemed to drain out of her from the very beginning. Of course, when the bloody bell would go, she would still say, 'The aul' bitch!' But, you know, even the way she said it now, like kind of weary, and almost as if it wasn't anger at the aul' woman at all but more to please me. That sort of thing. And a funny thing about the bloody bell, too. You know, before, if there was no noise coming from downstairs, that ringing would be enough to waken the dead. But *after* we got married, it only went when Hanna and me started talking. Wasn't that perverse now, eh? Oh, a deep one; deep as a well. We could sit, by God, for a whole night and not say a word to each other, and there wouldn't be a cheep from upstairs. But let us start chatting and the clanging would damn near shake the house! You know there, that sort of thing.

And then there was the Rosary caper. Well, I mean to say, a man has to draw the line somewhere. Oh, no, says I; we may have to stay together of necessity, says I, but by God it won't be because we pray together; I'll say my own mouthful of prayers down here. And that settled that. I mean to say, a man has to take a stand some time. No harm to Father U.S.A. Peyton, says I; but all things in their proper place, and the proper place for me and my missus is in Riverview. I'll manage rightly down here, says I; and Father Peyton and Saint Philomena and the three sorrowful mysteries can hammer away upstairs. She didn't like that, the aul' woman, I'll tell you. Didn't speak to me for weeks. And would you believe what she done on me to get her own back: it was Cissy told me with a wee toss of her head. 'She offered you up to Saint Philomena,' says she. Crafty? Oh, man! Hanna's thick — there's no denying that; but she'll never have the craft of the aul' woman.

But I got her! By God I got her! . . . or I damn near got her. It was this day in the works — a Friday — I'll never forget it — and George Williamson comes sidling up to me with a newspaper in his hand and a great aul' smirk on his jaw, and says he, 'So the Pope's not infallible after all, Andy,' says he. Oh, a bad bitter Protestant, the same Williamson. 'What's that?' says I, you know there, very quiet. 'According to the paper here,' says he, 'even the Pope can make a mistake. What d'you make of that now, eh? Isn't that a surprise?' And he hands me the paper. So I pulls out the glasses, very calm, and puts them on, and takes the paper from him and looks at it. And true as Christ, when I seen it, you could have tipped me over, I was that weak. Like, for five seconds, I couldn't even speak with excitement; only the heart thumping like bloody hell in my chest. For there it was in black and white before my very eyes: THE SAINT THAT NEVER WAS. 'Official Vatican sources today announced' — I know it by heart — 'that the devotion of all Roman Catholics to Saint Philomena must be discontinued at once because there is little or no evidence that such a person ever existed.' Like I never knew I was a spiteful man until that minute; and then, by God, my only thought was to stick that paper down the aul' woman's throat. Poor Williamson — Christ, I shot past him like a scalded cat and out of the workshop like the hammers of hell.

What I should have done — like, I know now — my God, no need to tell me; instead of coopering the things up the way I done — but what I should have done was wait until after the tea and then go upstairs nice and calm, you know there, and sit down on the side of the bed very pleasant, and say, 'Have a look through the paper there, Mrs. Wilson,' and watch, by God, watch every wee flicker of her eye when she'd come to the big news . . . but I bollixed it. I know. I know. I bollixed it. Straight from the workshop into a pub. And when closing time comes, there I am — blotto. And back to the house singing and shouting like a madman.

HANNA, *who has been in the bedroom, now removes the screen. And, as she does this,* ANDY *goes off.*
MRS WILSON *is in bed.* CISSY *is sitting on the edge of the bed.* HANNA *has been crying for some time and shuffles around the room, vaguely touching different things.*
The candles are lit. The atmosphere is subdued and

doleful and expectant. Trite words of consolation are being spoken. And one gets the sense of feminine solidarity and of suffering womanhood.

MRS WILSON I promise you, dear: he's all right. I know he is.

HANNA But where *is* he?

MRS WILSON Maybe he met some of his companions.

HANNA He has no companions.

MRS WILSON Maybe he's doing overtime.

HANNA There's no overtime this week.

MRS WILSON Or maybe he's gone to confession.

CISSY Ah! Indeed!

HANNA At half past ten? For God's sake!

MRS WILSON Well, we'll say the Rosary; that's what we'll do; and we'll ask God and Saint Philomena to look after us all. And before we're finished, you'll find he'll be home safe and sound to us.

CISSY Thanks be to God.

MRS WILSON All down on your knees. God and his holy mother guide all our thoughts and actions this day and this night. In the name of the Father and of the Son and of the Holy Ghost. The five sorrowful mysteries of the most holy Rosary —

Remote sounds of ANDY *singing.*

HANNA Sshhh!

MRS WILSON The first sorrowful mystery — the agony in the garden —

HANNA Sh! Sh! Listen! Listen!

The women freeze. Downstairs ANDY *staggers into the kitchen, singing* God Save Ireland. *The women are horrified.*

MRS WILSON Is it — ?

HANNA Shut up!

CISSY Singing! Andrew?

MRS WILSON He's not — ?

HANNA He is!

CISSY A drunk man!

> ANDY *flings his coat on the couch and reels to the bottom of the stairs. Calls up:*

ANDY Mrs. Wilson! Hello there, old mammy Wilson! I've got news for you . . . big, big news.

> HANNA *is terrified.* MRS WILSON *takes control.*

HANNA What in the name of God — ?

MRS WILSON Leave him to me.

ANDY Stay where you are till I come up . . . very important, old mammy . . . very important.

MRS WILSON Don't say a word. Leave everything to me.

CISSY Drunk — the dirty animal!

MRS WILSON Quiet.

HANNA But what if he — ?

MRS WILSON Don't worry. I'll settle him. And stop whinging!

> ANDY *enters and surveys the three alarmed faces. He has the newspaper in his hand.*

ANDY By God if it's not the Dolly Sisters! (*He gives them a grand bow*) And Saint Philomena! (*Grand bow to the statue*) All we need now is Father Peyton . . . Where's Father Peyton? . . . I'll tell you something: the family that drinks together sinks together.

MRS WILSON Andrew!

ANDY 'The cock's shrill clarion, or the echoing horn —'

CISSY Dirty animal!

ANDY 'No more shall rouse them from their lowly bed.
  For them no more the blazing hearth shall burn,
  Or busy housewife ply her evening care —'
  Thomas Gray, 1716 to 1771.

HANNA Mother, please —!

MRS WILSON Listen to me, Andrew!

ANDY She (HANNA) knows what I'm talking about 'cos she's my wife —

MRS WILSON If you don't behave yourself —

72

ANDY   As for prissy Cissy here —

CISSY   All for Thee — all for Thee —

ANDY   You'll go down with the white bobbins. Know what that means, prissy Cissy? The white bobbins? It means you'll never know your ass from your elbow.

HANNA   Andy!

MRS WILSON   I'll give you one minute to get out of this house —!

ANDY   News for you, old mammy — here, in this paper. (*To the statue*) And news for you, darling, too.

MRS WILSON   Get out!

ANDY   You've *(Philomena)* been sacked.

MRS WILSON   I said get out!

ANDY   *(To statue)* You and me — both sacked.

He comes over to the bed with the paper.

HANNA   Stop it, Andrew! Stop it!

ANDY   In black and white . . . Read it . . . It says: We don't stay together — that's what it says. Father Peyton, it says, your head's a marly. That's what it says.

CISSY   Dirty, dirty animal.

MRS WILSON   I warned you! I gave you ample warning! And if you think you can profane in this room —

She breaks off and clutches her heart and cries out.

CISSY   What — what is it?

HANNA   Mother! Mother?

ANDY *staggers back to the altar. On his way he kicks over the bell. He laughs.*

ANDY   'The curfew tolls no more the knell of parting day.' (*He lifts the statue and waltzes with it*) Come on, darling; we know when we're not wanted.

MRS WILSON   Don't — touch — that —

CISSY   The statue!

HANNA   Andrew!

CISSY   Oh, my God!

MRS WILSON   Stop him! Stop him!

Chaos and confusion as HANNA *and* CISSY *rush at* ANDY *and wrest the statue from him. Everyone is shouting at the same time.* MRS WILSON *gets out of bed and* CISSY *puts a coat round her.*

CISSY   Come on! Come on! Into my place!

HANNA   Are you all right, Mother?

ANDY   'Large was his bounty, and his soul sincere,
      Heav'n did a recompense as largely send —'

MRS WILSON   Take all — statue — candles — cloth —

CISSY   Brute animal!

MRS WILSON   Oh, my heart —

HANNA   Out — quick —

CISSY and HANNA *each take an arm of* MRS WILSON *and they support her out.* HANNA *also takes the altar things.* MRS WILSON *groans loudly and pathetically.* CISSY *consoles her.* ANDY *reels over to the bed and sits on it. He is muttering to himself.* HANNA *leaves the others, goes to him, and sticks her face into his, and hisses:*

HANNA   You'll regret this day, Andrew Tracey! You'll regret this day as long as you live!

She then pulls over the screen hiding ANDY *from view, and joins* CISSY *and her mother, who go off chattering hysterically.* ANDY *rises and watches them go.*

ANDY   (*Shouts after them from behind the screen*) We're sacked, Philomena — both of us — both sacked! What the hell are we going to do now? What the hell are we going to do now?

The three women have struggled downstairs and pause in the kitchen before escaping to CISSY'S *house.*

MRS WILSON   O my heart! O my God!

HANNA   How are you, Mother?

CISSY   All men is animals — brute aimals.

HANNA Come on, Mother. I'll look after you.
CISSY Brutes of the field.
MRS WILSON God have mercy on us this day and this night.
HANNA He'll pay for this. By God, he'll pay for this!

The three ladies go off.
ANDY appears, in cardigan and house slippers, and comes into the kitchen. He addresses the audience.

ANDY I don't think I told you about the tenant I have over in Riverview. Retired accountant. Quiet couple. No kids. He pays me on the first Saturday of every month. Sometimes if the weather's good I take an odd walk over there and look at the outside of the house. He has rose trees in the front and vegetables in the back. Very nice. Very cozy. But by the time you get home from work and get washed, you don't feel like going out much. So I usually sleep at the fire for a while and then come out here for a breath of air. Kills an hour or two. And then when the bell rings I go up to the aul' woman's room for the prayers. Well, I mean to say, anything for a quiet life. Hanna sleeps there now, as a matter of fact, just in case the aul' woman should get an attack during the night. Not that that's likely. The doctor says she'll go on forever.

And a funny thing, you know: nothing much has changed up there. Philomena's gone, of course. And she never mentions Father Peyton anymore. But she still has the altar and she still lights the candles and has the flowers in the middle and she still faces it when she's praying and mouths away to it. I asked Cissy about it one night when she came in — who the hell they were supposed to be praying to.

Enter CISSY in coat and hat. She is about to go straight upstairs but sees ANDY and pauses. She is very formal with him.

CISSY Good night, Andrew.
ANDY 'Night, Cissy.

75

CISSY The crowds for confession! You should see them. The poor priests must be mortified.

ANDY Cissy —

CISSY You'll be up later for the prayers?

ANDY I will. I will. Cissy —

CISSY Well?

ANDY Cissy, you've no statue up there now.

CISSY I'm not blind.

ANDY Well, I mean to say, what does she think she's at?

CISSY We've no statue, true enough; but we have a saint in our mind even though we've no figure for it.

HANNA enters. ANDY does not see her at first.

ANDY What saint?

CISSY Aha, that's something you'll never know, Andrew Tracey! Wild horses wouldn't drag that out of us. You robbed us of Saint Philomena but you'll never rob us of this one, for you'll never be told who it is!

CISSY marches upstairs and ANDY turns with embarrassment to HANNA. Her coldness to him is withering.

ANDY Damnit, she's fighting fit . . . isn't she? Hanna —

HANNA What?

ANDY Hanna, things are . . . we're not making . . . you and me, Hanna, we're not . . . Here, have a clove rock, Hanna.

She moves toward him as if she were going to take one, hesitates, then says:

HANNA No. They'd put me off my supper.

ANDY I suppose you're right.

HANNA You'll be up for the prayers?

ANDY I will . . . I will . . .

HANNA goes upstairs. ANDY turns to the audience and speaks with strained joviality.

ANDY And that's the way things are now. (*He goes slowly out toward the yard*) And when I go into the bedroom she smiles and nods at me and you can see her lips saying *Thank you, thank you* to the altar. And when we kneel down, she says, 'It's nice for me to have you all gathered round my bed. As a certain American cleric says: the family that prays together stays together.'

By God, you've got to admire the aul' bitch. She could handle a regiment.

He lifts the binoculars, puts them in front of his eyes, and stares at the wall in front of him.
Slowly bring down the lights until the stage is totally black.